Contents

KU-195-850

This is Spain!

Spain is a big country in the far west of Europe. Most people who come here on holiday arrive by aeroplane.

Spain is packed with fun places to visit. Look out for them in this book.

The **Canary Islands** and the **Balearic Islands** belong to Spain.

Santiago de Compostela

Atlantic Sea

FRANCE

Pyrenees mountains

Barcelona

Costa Brava

PORTUGAL

Madrid

SPAIN

Valencia

Balearic Islands

Córdoba

Seville

Canary Islands

Costa del Sol

Mediterranean Sea

ALGERIA

My Holiday in

Spain

...TON LIBRARY, ...
...H ON TRENT ...

Susie Brooks

WAYLAND

SCHOOLS LIBRARY SERVICE

3 8023 00549 1905

STAFFORDSHIRE
SCHOOLS LIBRARY SERVICE

3 8023 00549 190 5	
PET	19-Jan-2011
C914.6	£7.99
XSLS	

First published in 2008 by Wayland

This paperback edition published in 2010 by Wayland

Copyright © Wayland 2008

Wayland
338 Euston Road
London NW1 3BH

Wayland Australia
Level 17/207 Kent Street
Sydney NSW 2000

All rights reserved.

Senior Editor: Claire Shanahan
Designer: Elaine Wilkinson
Map artwork: David le Jars

Brooks, Susie

My holiday in Spain
 1. Vacations - Spain - Juvenile literature 2. Recreation -
Spain - Juvenile literature 3. Spain - Juvenile literature
4. Spain - Social life and customs - Juvenile literature
I. Title II. Spain
914.6'0483

ISBN 978 0 7502 6368 9

Cover: the Sagrada Familia Church, Barcelona, © Tom Grill/Corbis; sightseeing boats on coast of
Ibiza, Spain, © Manfred Mehlig/Getty.

p5: © Tim Pannell/Corbis; p6: © Jose Fuste Raga/Corbis; p7: © John Eder/Getty; p8: © Hans Georg Roth/Corbis;
p9: © Arne Pastoor/Getty; p10: © Don Klumpp/Getty; p11: © Rob Cousins/Robert Harding World Imagery/Corbis;
p12: © Michael Busselle/Robert Harding World Imagery/Corbis; p13: © Manfred Mehlig/Getty; p14: © Dusko
Despotovic/Corbis; p15: © Jeremy Green/Alamy; p16: © Tom Grill/Corbis; p17: © Michael Busselle/Corbis; p18:
© Alan Copson/JAI/Corbis; p19: © Martin Barraud/Getty; p20: © Martin Barraud/Getty; p21: © Ian
Dagnall/Alamy; p22: © Nik Wheeler/Corbis; p23: © Claire Shanahan; p24: © Jochem D Wijnands/Getty; p25:
Demetrio Carrasco © Rough Guides; p26, title page: © Bob Krist/Corbis; p27: © Claire Shanahan; © Jerry
Cooke/Corbis; p28: © Reuters/Corbis; p29: © Pete Saloutos/Corbis; © Harry Rhodes/Wishlist Images 2008; p30:
© wen Franken/ Corbis.

Printed in China

Wayland is a division of Hachette Children's Books, an Hachette UK company.

www.hachette.co.uk

It's fun to take a camera to Spain.

Arriving in Spain is exciting. Look and listen for things that are different from home. For a start, you will need to change the time on your watch.

The Spanish people speak really fast!

Speak Spanish!

hello/hi
hola (**o**-la)

please
por favor (por-fa-**bvor**)

thank you
gracias (**gra**-thee-ass)

Summer sun

If you visit Spain in summer, it is almost certain to be hot. Some parts of the country get hotter than others — check the weather forecast before you go!

Lots of holidaymakers head for Spain's sunny beaches. This is Tossa de Mar on the Costa Brava.

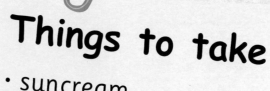

Things to take

- suncream
- sun hat
- swimming costume
- bucket and spade

If you're not near the seaside, an aqua park is a great place to cool off!

Madrid, the capital of Spain, can be scorching in the summer months. In July and August, many people move away to cooler places near the coast or in the mountains.

Winter fun

Spain is a good place to visit in winter – parts of the country stay quite warm. In the far south and on the Canary Islands, you'll find sunshine all year round.

You can ride a camel on black sand on Lanzarote in the Canary Islands.

Winter in the mountains is cold and snowy. You can go to the beach in the morning and get to the mountains by the afternoon – but don't forget a change of clothes!

Skiing is popular in the Pyrenees mountains in northern Spain.

Speak Spanish!

sun
sol (sol)

snow
nieve (nee-**ye**-bay)

beach
playa (**ply**-ya)

A place to stay

Spain is dotted with pretty towns and villages.

Lots of people who visit Spain stay in city hotels or **apartments** near the sea. Holiday houses called villas are popular too, usually in quieter spots.

Speak Spanish!

house
casa (ca-sa)
bed
cama (ca-ma)
bathroom
baño (**ban**-yo)

You could stay in a house with a roof terrace, a tent near the beach or even a giant castle!

Some people in the Spanish countryside live in cave houses.

 I got in a muddle with the taps – they had different letters on! In Spain, C is hot (caliente) and F is cold (frio).

On the move

Driving around Spain is a good way to see the country. People drive on the right-hand side of the road. They toot their horns when they overtake.

In the Spanish countryside, farmers often use donkeys to carry their loads.

We drove through the mountains. The roads were really wiggly and I felt a bit sick!

These **tourist** boats are taking people to a beach on the Balearic island of Ibiza.

To get to the Spanish islands, it is quickest to fly. Some people take a ferry to the Balearic Islands, or sail a yacht around the coasts.

Speak Spanish!

car
coche (**co**-chay)

boat
barco (**bar**-co)

train
tren (tren)

Amazing Madrid

Imagine living in the Royal Palace – it has 2,800 rooms! This is the Grand Dining Hall.

Madrid, Spain's capital city, is right in the middle of the country. It is busy, noisy and full of things to see.

People in Madrid like to spend time in the city parks and squares. There are often musicians, puppet shows and other acts to entertain them.

There's a fun park and zoo at the Casa del Campo. You can get there by cable car.

Don't miss

El Prado – a massive art museum

Plaza Mayor – the lively main square, with cafés and musicians

Parque Mágico – a park with bumper boats and a mini race track

15

Magical buildings

For spectacular buildings, visit Barcelona! A famous Spanish **architect** called Gaudi lived here. Look for his fairytale houses and the Sagrada Familia church.

You can tell why some people call the Sagrada Familia the sandcastle church!

Climbing up inside the Sagrada Familia made me really dizzy— there was a twisty staircase with 400 steps!

This mosque in Córdoba is now used as a Christian church.

There are beautiful holy buildings in many other cities too, including Seville, León and Santiago de Compostela. Most people in Spain are members of the **Roman Catholic** religion.

Every year, lots of people walk for weeks to visit the cathedral at Santiago de Compostela.

Feeling hungry

Tasting new foods is part of the holiday adventure! A fun thing to eat in Spain is tapas. You get to try lots of snack-size dishes, from spicy meats to sweet treats.

Don't miss churros con chocolate – you dip doughnuts into thick hot chocolate.

Paella is made up of rice, meat and seafood, cooked together in a big pan.

Paella is Spain's national dish. The Spanish people eat a lot of fish and seafood. They like to cook with plenty of garlic and olive oil – you will smell it!

On the menu

chorizo (cho-**ree**-tho) - **spicy sausage**

tortilla (tor-**tee**-ya) - **potato omelette**

pan (pan) - **bread**

Family time

After lunch there is a break called a **siesta**, when many shops close and it is traditional to have a rest.

Spanish families love spending time together.

zzzZZZZZZ

Dinner is usually eaten after 9pm, so bedtime is late even for the children!

In the evening, city streets come to life with families out and about having fun.

We went out shopping in the evening and I got to stay up till 11pm!

Speak Spanish!

family
familia (fa-**mee**-lee-ya)

mum
madre (**ma**-dray)

dad
padre (**pa**-dray)

21

Let's go shopping

Markets are some of the best places for shopping in Spain. Look out for colourful stalls of fruits and vegetables that are grown in the Spanish countryside.

On a Sunday, the enormous Rastro market in Madrid sells everything from old clothes to wild animals!

The money you spend in Spain is called the euro. Try to buy something you can bring home as a **souvenir**.

Spain is famous for its hand-painted pottery. Pick your favourite piece!

Speak Spanish!

shop
tienda (tee-**yen**-da)

market
mercado (mare-**ca**-do)

money
dinero (din-**air**-ro)

In the wild

Spain is full of wide open spaces where farm animals and wild animals roam.

Visit the Doñana National Park and you might spot a rare Iberian lynx.

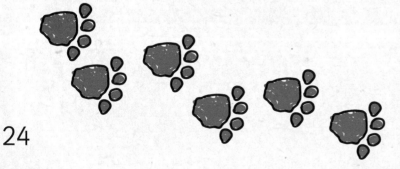

Look out for

flamingos – Andalusia

monkeys – Gibraltar

ibex (mountain goats) – Pyrenees

dolphins – in the sea!

It's fun to go for a bike ride, pony trek or camping trip in the hills of **Andalusia**. You'll see lots of olive trees. Further south in Almeria, the land is very hot and dry, like a desert.

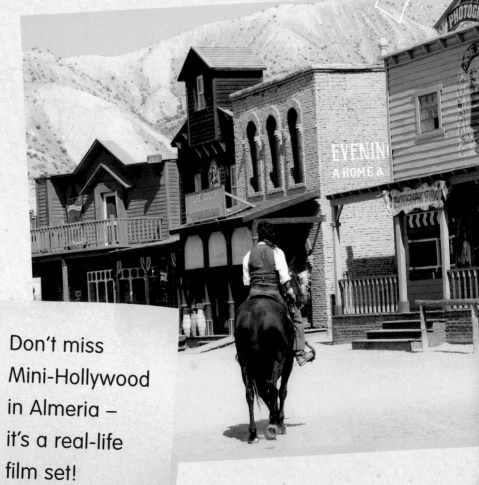

Don't miss Mini-Hollywood in Almeria – it's a real-life film set!

Be a sport!

It doesn't take long to notice that Spanish people are crazy about football! Watersports, mountain biking and basketball are also popular.

Learning to windsurf is exciting in the Spanish sun!

We went to watch a football match at the Barca stadium in Barcelona. It was so massive it took us ages to find our seats!

Bullfighting has taken place in Spain for hundreds of years. This fight is in Seville.

Bullfighting is a traditional Spanish pastime that some people think is cruel. Most cities in Spain have a bullring with thousands of seats.

This poster is for a bullfight in Benalmadena in southern Spain.

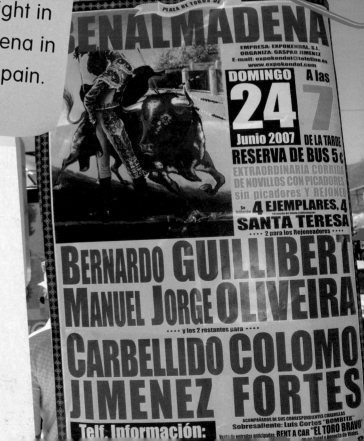

PLAZA DE TOROS DE

BENALMADENA

EMPRESA: EXPOKENDAL, S.L.
ORGANIZA: GASPAR JIMENEZ
E-mail: expokendal@toteline.es
www.expokendal.com

DOMINGO A las

24 7

Junio 2007 DE LA TARDE

RESERVA DE BUS 5 €

EXTRAORDINARIA CORRIDA
DE NOVILLOS CON PICADORES
sin picadores Y REJONEO

4 EJEMPLARES, 4
SANTA TERESA

···· 2 para los Rejoneadores ····

BERNARDO GUILLIBERT
MANUEL JORGE OLIVEIRA

···· y los 2 restantes para ····

CARBELLIDO COLOMO
JIMENEZ FORTES

ACOMPAÑADOS DE SUS CORRESPONDIENTES CUADRILLAS
Sobresaliente: Luis Cortes "BOMBITA"
RENT A CAR "EL TORO BRAVO"

Telf. Información:

Venta de entradas anticipadas:

Party time

Many people try to visit Spain during a festival, or fiesta. Fiestas happen all over the country, and each region has its own special party.

At Tomatina in Buñol near Valencia, people throw tomatoes at each other for fun!

Fiestas often include **flamenco** dancers. They stamp their feet, twirl around and play little wooden instruments called **castanets**.

Flamenco dancers wear fancy costumes. Listen for the click of their castanets!

Famous fiestas

Cabalgata de Reyes (countrywide, January)	Las Fallas (Valencia, March)	San Fermin (Pamplona, July)	
Three Wise Men throw sweets at the crowds	people set fire to giant papier mâché figures	men run through the streets chased by bulls	

Play it yourself

Try this Spanish playground game! It is a simple version of pelota pared, a sport invented in the Basque region of northern Spain.

In real pelota, people hit the ball with special bats strapped to their hands.

Pelota pared (wall ball)

You will need:

- a tennis ball
- chalk
- an outside wall
- 2 or more players.

1. Draw a chalk line across the wall, at about waist height.

2. Player 1 bounces the ball once, then hits it using a bare hand at the wall above the chalk line.

3. Player 2 lets the returning ball bounce once on the ground, then hits it back at the wall in the same way.

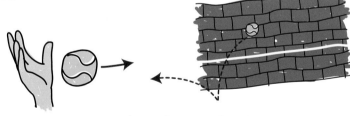

4. Players take turns as above.

You are OUT if the ball bounces more than once on the ground or the ball hits the wall below the chalk line.

TIP: You could play with five lives – one for each letter of the word burro (Spanish for donkey)!

Useful words

Andalusia	An area in southern Spain.
apartment	A room or flat.
architect	Someone who designs buildings.
Balearic Islands	A group of Spanish islands, including Majorca and Ibiza, which lie to the east of Spain.
Canary Islands	A group of Spanish islands, including Lanzarote and Tenerife, which lie off the north-west coast of Africa.
castanets	Small musical instruments made from two hinged pieces of wood that the player clicks together in one hand.
flamenco	A traditonal type of Spanish music and dance that was invented in Andalusia.
Roman Catholic	A type of Christian. Roman Catholics worship in churches and cathedrals.
siesta	The Spanish afternoon break, usually taken between 2pm and 5pm.
souvenir	Something you take home to remind you of somewhere you have been.
tourist	Someone who is on holiday or sightseeing.